Producer: Moo Media Publications Limited

Would You Rather? Grown-up Edition:
400+ outrageous, thought-provoking, and slightly close-to-the-bone questions for people ready and willing to speak the truth.

ISBN:

Welcome to the Would You Rather Grown-up Edition.

The ultimate game book that pushes the boundaries of fun, surpises, and unexpected revelations. Whether you're hosting a party, enjoying a night in with friends, or simply looking for a way to break the ice, this book is your perfect companion.

Inside these pages, you'll find a collection of "Would You Rather?" questions that range from the hilariously awkward to the wildly outrageous. We've curated scenarios that will make you think, laugh, and maybe even blush.

These questions are designed to spark conversations, reveal hidden truths, and create unforgettable moments.

Expect to learn things about each other you never anticipated...

The Rules (Boring But Necessary)

Welcome to "Would You Rather?" – the game that takes you from the awkward to the outrageous! Gather your friends (while they're still your friends), grab some snacks, and get ready for some home truths and unexpected reveals. Here are the rules to keep the fun flowing and everyone engaged:

1. **Pick Your Moderator:** Kick things off by selecting a moderator – the master of ceremonies! They'll read each question aloud, keep the turns in order, and ensure the game flows smoothly. Rotate this role if you want everyone to get a chance to spill the beans.

2. **Hear Ye, Hear Ye!:** The moderator picks a juicy question from the book and reads it out loud to the group. Make sure everyone's listening – no secrets allowed!

3. Take Your Turn: Players take turns answering the question. Go around in a circle or let the moderator mix it up. Remember, you must choose one of the two options – "neither" and "both" are off the table!

4. The Whole Truth And Nothing But The Truth: After answering, dive into why you chose your option. This is where the magic happens – hilarious explanations, wild stories, and passionate debates!

5. Wild Card Power: Got a question that's too hot to handle? Use your "Wild Card" to skip it without penalty. But choose wisely – each player only gets one Wild Card per game!

6. Keep the Banter Going: The moderator can ask follow-up questions to stir the pot and keep the chat lively. Share your wildest thoughts, funniest anecdotes, and craziest ideas!

7. Respect the Vibe: Be cool and respect everyone's comfort zones. If a player wants to use their Wild Card or pass on a detail, let them. We're here for fun, not discomfort!

8. Move It Along: To keep the energy high, the moderator can set a time limit for each question or round. This keeps things snappy and ensures everyone gets a shot.

9. Vote for Fun: Feeling competitive? After everyone's answered and explained, vote on the most interesting or funniest explanation. The moderator counts the votes and announces the winner – just for kicks!

10. End with a Bang: Wrap up the game with a bang! Choose the funniest or most outrageous question for the grand finale, ensuring everyone leaves with a big smile.

Example Game Flow:

Moderator: "Would you rather accidentally send a sexy text to your boss or a nude photo to your mom?"

Player 1: "I'd rather send the sexy text to my boss. At least I can try to laugh it off as a joke gone wrong. Plus, it might lead to an interesting conversation!"

Player 2: "I'd go with the nude photo to my mom. She already changed my diapers; she's seen it all. It would be mortifying, but she'd forgive me eventually."

Player 3: "I'd choose the sexy text to my boss. I'd frame it as an autocorrect disaster and hope for the best!"

Moderator: "Great answers! Player 1, what would be your go-to excuse for sending that text to your boss?"

Example Game Flow:

Moderator: "Would you rather have a parrot that constantly insults you in public or a dog that humps everyone's leg at the worst times?"

Player 1: "I'd rather have the insulting parrot because I can at least teach it some creative comebacks and become a viral sensation."

Player 2: "I'd choose the humping dog. It's embarrassing, but it could lead to some hilarious stories and maybe even a reality TV show!"

Player 3: "I'd go with the parrot too. At least it's easier to carry a parrot around and pretend it's part of a comedy act!"

Moderator: "Fantastic answers! Player 2, what would be the title of your reality TV show with the humping dog?"

Career
Conundrums

Would you rather have your work performance judged by your internet browsing history or your most recent drunk texts?

Would you rather work in a job where you get paid well but have to wear an embarrassing costume every day, or a low-paying job with a wear what you like policy?

Would you rather have a job where you must give presentations naked or where you have to present to a naked audience?

Would you rather work 80 hours a week doing something you love or 40 hours a week doing something you hate?

Would you rather work in a place where everyone can hear your bathroom noises or where everyone can smell them?

Would you rather be a respected but underpaid professor or a highly paid but publically ridiculed reality TV star?

Would you rather deal with a coworker who constantly talks about their personal problems or one who never showers?

Would you rather work for a company with no vacation days but high pay or one with unlimited vacation but very low pay?

Would you rather be the CEO of a successful company with a terrible reputation or an employee of a failing company with a stellar reputation?

Would you rather be known as the office gossip or the office snitch?

Would you rather have a job where you have to work with your ex or where you can only communicate with coworkers through emojis?

Would you rather have a job that requires you to lie every day or one that requires you to tell brutal truths?

Would you rather have an incredibly attractive boss who is completely incompetent or a highly competent boss who is unbearably unattractive?

Would you rather always have to wear a tuxedo or ballgown in a smart-casual office environment or always have to wear a hat that says "I'm the Boss," even though you're not?

Would you rather have a job where you can only use the bathroom at designated times or one where the bathroom is always out of toilet paper?

Love
Hurts

Would you rather accidentally call your partner by your ex's name during sex or have them do the same to you?

Would you rather have your partner read your mind during intimate moments or be able to read theirs?

Would you rather accidentally send a nude photo to your partner's parents or have them accidentally send one to you?

Would you rather have a partner who talks dirty to you in public or one who insists you talk dirty to them?

Would you rather find out your mum had a secret OnlyFans account or your partner was an OnlyFans addict?

Would you rather your mother walk in on you while you're watching porn or your father?

Would you rather have to discuss your sexual history in every detail with your partner's best friend or hear all about theirs?

Would you rather have your partner be incredibly kinky but have no sense of humor or be hilariously funny but very vanilla in bed?

Would you rather accidentally send your partner a text meant for your crush or receive one from them meant for theirs?

Would you rather have a partner who is obsessed with taking selfies during sex or one who will only have sex with the light off?

Would you rather have to narrate your feelings during every intimate moment out loud or have your partner narrate theirs?

Would you rather have a partner who is terrible in bed but amazing at everything else or one who is incredible in bed but awful at everything else?

Would you rather have a partner who fakes orgasms after a certain time or one who insists on keeping going until they orgasm even if you're long over it?

Would you rather have your partner only be able to turn you on with really bad jokes or really bad dancing?

Would you rather have to wear a shock collar during sex that your partner controls or have them wear one that you control?

Would you rather have your partner talk to you in a baby voice during sex or in a foreign accent?

Would you rather have your partner tell your deepest sexual secrets to their best friend or your worst enemy?

Would you rather have to narrate your sexual encounters out loud or have them live-streamed without sound?

Would you rather your neighbors always hear you having sex or you always hear them?

Would you rather have sex with your ex once a year or never have sex again?

Would you rather have sex with a stranger in front of your partner or have your partner have sex with a stranger in front of you?

Would you rather have sex with someone who insists on dirty talk but is terrible at it or someone who remains completely silent, even during orgasm?

Wanderlust

Would you rather be stuck on a 12-hour flight next to a screaming baby or next to a passenger with terrible body odor?

Would you rather accidentally send your most embarrassing travel photo to your boss or your parents?

Would you rather have to hitchhike across a country with your annoying relative or with your partner's ex?

Would you rather have food poisoning on a romantic getaway with a new partner or food poisoning on an adventure trek in the middle of the jungle?

Would you rather accidentally book a nude beach resort with your dad or with your boss?

Would you rather have to wear the same underwear for a week while traveling or no underwear at all?

Would you rather accidentally walk in on your parents during their romantic getaway or have them walk in on you during yours?

Would you rather get caught in a compromising position by hotel staff or accidentally walk in on the hotel staff in a compromising position in your room?

Would you rather have your romantic dinner interrupted by a loud and obnoxious bachelorette party or be serenaded throughout by an overjealous performer?

Would you rather share a hostel room with a couple having loud sex or with someone who snores like a chainsaw?

Would you rather accidentally post a video of yourself skinny dipping on social media or have someone else post it and tag you?

Would you rather forget to pack any toiletries or forget to pack any clothes?

Would you rather have to explain a sex toy in your luggage to customs or explain a bag full of exotic spices that look suspicious?

Would you rather have to take a cold outdoor shower every day of your trip or have to use a toilet with no privacy?

Would you rather be photobombed by a stranger in all your travel photos or have a stranger photoshop themselves into your photos after the trip?

Would you rather stay in a luxury hotel that's haunted or a budget hostel?

Would you rather miss your flight and be stuck in an airport for 24 hours or arrive at your destination with no luggage?

Health Hijinks

Would you rather accidentally fart loudly during yoga class or loudly burp while lifting weights at the gym?

Would you rather have to wear a bright neon spandex outfit to the public gym or work out naked in a private gym?

Would you rather only be able to eat bland, healthy food and never have to work out again or eat delicious junk food and have to work out everyday?

Would you rather have your personal trainer be extremely attractive but very strict and derogatory about your body or unattractive but incredibly encouraging?

Would you rather have to post every workout session on social media or have to share every meal you eat?

Would you rather have to exercise in front of a huge mirror or in front of a live audience?

Would you rather have to take a freezing cold shower after every workout at the gym or not shower at all?

Would you rather be forced to do a juice cleanse for a week or eat nothing but raw vegetables for a month?

Would you rather accidentally wear see-through leggings to the gym or have your shorts split during a workout class?

Would you rather give up your favorite food forever or have to do an extreme workout every day for the rest of your life?

Would you rather always have to work out next to someone who grunts loudly or someone who constantly checks themselves out in the mirror?

Would you rather have your workout live-streamed to your colleagues once a week or have a public weigh-in in the office canteen?

Would you rather always have visible sweat stains or a red face after working out?

Would you rather have to join a workout class where everyone is much fitter than you or where everyone is a complete beginner?

Would you rather have to run a mile with diarrhea or do hot yoga with a massive hangover?

Would you rather have to eat a live worm after every workout or drink a smoothie made of your sweat?

Would you rather have to work out with a celebrity trainer who hates you or a local personal trainer who is obsessed with you?

Would you rather have to take a fitness class that's way too advanced for you or one that's way too easy?

Dollar Dillemas

Would you rather inherit a fortune from a relative but they insist on being buried in your backyard or receive a modest inheritance and bury your relative in a cematory?

Would you rather have to ask your parents for money every month or take out high-interest payday loans?

Would you rather win the lottery but have to spend a year in prison or live debt-free but never be able to save any money

Would you rather have to donate a large sum of money to a cause you disagree with or lose the same amount gambling?

Would you rather have to take a job cleaning porta-potties for a year or spend a month living in one to receive a large cash prize?

Would you rather have your credit card declined at a fancy restaurant in front of important clients or find out your identity was stolen and all your accounts drained?

Would you rather have to beg for money on the streets for a week or work as a butler for a hated rival?

Would you rather invest in a shady business deal that could make you forever rich or a secure investment that guarantees modest returns?

Would you rather have to live a year without any money or live a year without any friends or family?

Would you rather win a billion dollars but everyone you know finds out all your deepest secrets or win a modest amount but keep your privacy?

Would you rather have to sell all your possessions to pay off debt or secretly steal to maintain your lifestyle?

Would you rather have to declare bankruptcy and start over or work two minimum-wage jobs to stay afloat?

Would you rather have a rich partner who is controlling or a poor partner who gives you complete freedom?

Would you rather live in luxury with the constant fear of losing it all or live modestly with complete financial security?

Would you rather have to disclose your entire financial history to your boss or to your partner's parents?

Would you rather have a million dollars but never be able to travel again or be broke but able to travel the world for free?

Would you rather have to sell your dream house to pay off debt or take a second mortgage and risk losing everything?

Would you rather have to explain every expense to a frugal partner or have a partner who spends lavishly without consulting you?

Would you rather have to split all your earnings with an annoying coworker or take a pay cut to work alone?

Would you rather win a million dollars but lose all your current friends or stay in your current financial situation with all your friends?

Would you rather have to spend a month doing extreme couponing to afford basic necessities or spend a month living off the grid with no money at all?

Ethical Escapades

Would you rather help a friend cover up a drunken one-night stand or confess to their partner yourself?

Would you rather tell your friend their cooking is terrible or pretend to love it and suffer through every meal?

Would you rather reveal an embarrassing secret about yourself to save a friend from humiliation or let your friend take the fall?

Would you rather have your child be the most popular kid in school for all the wrong reasons or be the least popular but for a good reason?

Would you rather have to publicly apologize for a racist joke you didn't make or laugh at one to avoid social awkwardness?

Would you rather have to donate to a cause you despise or refuse to donate and be labeled as heartless?

Would you rather have your child think you're perfect and find out you're not or know all your flaws from the start?

Would you rather have to fake being sick to get out of a wedding or attend the wedding and accidentally ruin it with a drunken speech?

Would you rather be caught lying on your resume or get a job you're completely unqualified for and risk being exposed?

Would you rather accidentally share a controversial opinion on social media or stay silent and let a friend post something offensive on your behalf?

Would you rather have to fake being religious to please your partner's family or admit your true beliefs and risk their disapproval?

Would you rather have to tell a stranger their fly is down or that they have toilet paper stuck to their shoe?

Would you rather have to choose between your child getting into a prestigious school through unethical means or them going to a underperforming school without cheating the system?

Would you rather have to fake enthusiasm for your friend's singing abilities and let them humiliate themselves on X-factor or honestly tell them they need more practice at the risk of your friendship?

Would you rather have to discipline someone else's child in public or have another parent discipline your child in front of you?

Starstruck Shenanigans

Would you rather accidentally insult your favorite celebrity to their face or be publicly insulted by them on social media?

Would you rather have an awkward one-night stand with a celebrity and it becomes tabloid news or accidentally walk in on them during an intimate moment with your partner?

Would you rather have to sing a duet with a tone-deaf celebrity or dance with one who has two left feet on live TV?

Would you rather have a celebrity you idolize block you on social media or have them follow you and see all your embarrassing posts?

Would you rather have to reveal your most embarrassing secret to a famous talk show host or watch your parents argue about their affairs on a tabloid talk show?

Would you rather be mistaken for a paparazzi and chased by a celebrity or have a celebrity mistake you for their assistant and boss you around?

Would you rather get caught taking a sneaky selfie with a celebrity or have them catch you gossiping about them?

Would you rather have to eat dinner with a celebrity you despise or publicly praise their worst movie?

Would you rather have to tell a famous chef their food is terrible or pretend to love a dish that makes you sick?

Would you rather get stuck in an elevator with a celebrity you have a crush on and embarrass yourself or with a celebrity who has a crush on you and embarrass them?

Would you rather receive a terrible makeover from a famous stylist or give a terrible makeover to a famous actor?

Would you rather be caught on camera photobombing a celebrity's perfect shot or have them photobomb all your important moments?

Would you rather be interviewed live on TV about a celebrity scandal you know nothing about or have to pretend to be that celebrity for a day?

Would you rather have a one-night stand with a celebrity and have to deal with the paparazzi aftermath or be rumored to have slept with a celebrity you never met?

Would you rather receive a sexy DM from a celebrity and accidentally screenshot it to your story or accidentally send a sexy DM to a celebrity and have them screenshot it?

Would you rather have a famous celebrity write a tell-all book about your intimate encounters or have them release a diss track about you?

Tech Tangles

Would you rather have to use a flip phone with no Internet access for a year or have your current smartphone but with a cracked screen that means you can only see half the screen?

Would you rather always have a 5-second delay on everything you say in a video call or have your camera freeze on the most unflattering expressions?

Would you rather have to deal with a computer virus that sends random embarrassing emails or one that deletes your important files?

Would you rather have to use a dial-up internet connection for a month or have no internet connection at all for a week

Would you rather your phone battery only lasts for 1 hour each day or your phone gets stuck at 10% brightness forever?

Would you rather have a laptop that overheats and shuts down frequently or one with a keyboard that sticks and types random letters?

Would you rather have all your selfies automatically uploaded to a public website or have every text message you send published in a local newspaper

Would you rather your favorite social media account get hacked and post embarrassing content or lose all your followers overnight?

Would you rather have to use a traditional typewriter for all your documents or write everything by hand, including emails

Would you rather have your favorite app replaced with a prank version or have your alarm clock app fail every time you have an important meeting?

Would you rather have your smart fridge announce your diet failures to your entire household or have it randomly lock and unlock itself?

Would you rather have your phone autocorrect all your texts to something inappropriate or never be able to use autocorrect again?

Would you rather your smart watch send all your health data to your boss or post it on your social media?

Would you rather have your laptop's fan sound like a jet engine on a busy train or have it overheat every 30 minutes?

Would you rather have your internet search history shared with your nosy neighbor or have your most embarrassing moments turned into memes?

Social Snafus

Would you rather accidentally call someone by the wrong name for an entire evening or forget their name and have to ask them multiple times?

Would you rather have a wardrobe malfunction at a big party or spill a drink on the host's expensive carpet?

Would you rather accidentally send a gossipy text to the person you're gossiping about or accidentally post it on social media?

Would you rather have to attend a party where you know no one or host a party where no one shows up?

Would you rather have an awkward conversation with an ex at a friend's wedding or run into them at a romantic getaway with your new partner?

Would you rather laugh uncontrollably at a funeral or cry uncontrollably at a wedding?

Would you rather loudly fart during a quiet meeting or have your stomach growl loudly during an important presentation?

Would you rather give a speech while needing to use the bathroom or while having a terrible itch you can't scratch?

Would you rather have to apologize for something embarrassing you did while drunk or something you said sober in confidence that was overheard?

Would you rather have to make a heartfelt toast at a stranger's wedding or perform a stand-up comedy routine at your boss's birthday party?

Would you rather accidentally insult someone you idolise's cooking at a dinner party or tell an inappropriate joke in front of the Pope?

Would you rather be stuck in an hour-long conversation with someone who spits while talking or someone with terrible breath?

Would you rather have to wear a revealing outfit to a conservative event or an overly formal outfit to a casual gathering?

Would you rather your significant other tell a highly embarrassing story about you to your friends or your parents do it at a family gathering?

Would you rather have to deal with an obvious wardrobe malfunction in public or walk around with toilet paper stuck to your shoe all day?

Would you rather be the only sober person at a wild party or the only drunk person at a very formal event?

Would you rather have to tell a coworker their fly is down or that they have something stuck in their teeth?

Would you rather accidentally walk into the wrong bathroom at a crowded event or get locked in a bathroom stall during an important event?

Would you rather have to give a speech with a huge zit on your face or with food stuck in your teeth?

Would you rather have your crush catch you picking your nose or fart loudly in front of them?

Would you rather be the person who always interrupts others or the person who is always interrupted?

Would you rather be caught mocking someone behind their back or have them mock you without realizing you're listening?

Would you rather have to talk to someone who stands way too close or someone who keeps backing away?

Would you rather be known as the person who is always dull or the person who is always drunk?

Would you rather have to sit through an entire dinner with someone who chews loudly or someone who talks with their mouth full?

Would you rather have to attend a high school reunion where no one remembers you or one where everyone remembers your most embarrassing moment?

Would you rather be the only person not invited to the unpopular coworker's party or the only person who shows up to it?

Would you rather be caught doing the chicken dance at a wedding or singing off-key at karaoke night?

Parenting Perils

Would you rather accidentally send a sext meant for your partner to your child's teacher or receive one from them?

Would you rather have to chaperone your child's awkward school dance or their rebellious teenage party?

Would you rather find out your child has been secretly skipping school or that they've been telling their teacher all your family secrets?

Would you rather have to apologize to your child's teacher for your own behavior or for your child's misbehavior?

Would you rather be caught gossiping about another parent by your child's teacher or by the parent you were gossiping about?

Would you rather be known as the overly strict parent or the overly lenient parent among your child's teachers?

Would you rather have your child's teacher critique your parenting style in front of other parents or have your child criticize you in front of their teacher?

Would you rather have your child's friends walk in on you during an intimate moment or have their teacher catch you in a compromising situation at a school event?

Would you rather have your child's teacher see your embarrassing social media posts or accidentally post something inappropriate on the school's social media account?

Would you rather attend parents' evening in an embarrassing outfit or belch loudly during your child's school performance?

Would you rather be caught sneaking a drink at a school event or sneaking a peek at other children's grades in the teacher's diary?

Would you rather have to sit through a painfully awkward sex education class taught by your child's teacher or teach it yourself in front of your child's class?

Would you rather have your child's teacher find out about your wild college days or your current embarrassing hobby?

Would you rather accidentally reveal a family secret during parents' evening or have your child reveal it during show-and-tell?

Would you rather have your child's teacher confront you about a private argument they overheard you have with another parent or about the names you have been calling other children?

Would you rather have to explain to your child why you got into a heated argument with their teacher or why you got overly friendly with their teacher?

Feast or Fumble

Would you rather have to eat a live insect or drink a glass of spoiled milk?

Would you rather be forced to eat only bland food for a month or incredibly spicy food for a week?

Would you rather eat a meal that tastes great but looks disgusting or a meal that looks great but tastes terrible?

Would you rather have to eat a whole raw onion or a whole lemon?

Would you rather be forced to eat the same meal every day for a year or never eat the same meal twice in a year?

Would you rather have to eat food that's always a bit undercooked or food that's always a bit burnt?

Would you rather always have to eat with your hands or always have to use chopsticks, even for soup?

Would you rather have to eat something you dropped on the floor or something you found in the back of the fridge?

Would you rather eat a food that makes your breath smell awful or one that makes you burp constantly?

Would you rather have to lick every plate clean after eating or have to drink all the leftover drinks at a party?

Would you rather eat a dish prepared by someone who doesn't wash their hands or one prepared by someone who cooks while naked?

Would you rather have to eat a meal that's been licked by a pet or one that's been sneezed on by a stranger?

Growth Gauntlet

Would you rather have to give up social media for a year or give up watching TV and movies for a year?

Would you rather read one book every week for a year or write a book in one year?

Would you rather attend a motivational seminar by your least favorite speaker or take a class taught by your most boring teacher?

Would you rather have to meditate for an hour every day or do intense physical exercise for an hour every day?

Would you rather face your biggest fear once or have minor annoyances daily for a year?

Would you rather have to apologize to someone you wronged years ago or forgive someone who wronged you and never apologized?

Would you rather have to take a cold shower every morning or run a mile every morning?

Would you rather go a year without any junk food or a year without any form of alcohol?

Would you rather have to be completely honest about your thoughts and feelings for a week or keep all your thoughts and feelings to yourself for a month?

Would you rather take a vow of silence for a week or a vow of no internet for a month?

Would you rather take a vow of celibacy for a year or take a vow of honesty for a year where you can't tell a single lie

Would you rather have to attend a week-long silent retreat or a week-long retreat with no personal boundaries?

Would you rather give up sex for a year to achieve your biggest goal or achieve your biggest goal but have everyone think you cheated to get there?

Would you rather spend a week in isolation with no human contact or a week being constantly surrounded by people without a moment alone?

Would you rather have to apologize to someone you've wronged face-to-face or publicly in a viral video?

Would you rather be forced to make a major life decision on impulse or be unable to make any decisions without consulting a group of strangers?

Would you rather have to live with your parents for the rest of your life or never be able to visit them again?

Would you rather give up all physical pleasure for a year or have to share a detailed account of your sexual exploits via an online diary.

Spooky Scenarios

Would you rather spend a night in a haunted house with a friendly ghost or in a house with no ghosts but lots of creepy noises?

Would you rather have the ability to see ghosts but not communicate with them or communicate with ghosts but never see them?

Would you rather be haunted by a ghost that only appears in mirrors or one that only appears in your dreams?

Would you rather turn into a werewolf every full moon or turn into a bat every night?

Would you rather be abducted by aliens once and returned safely or have minor paranormal experiences every night?

Would you rather have a vampire as a roommate or a zombie as a neighbor?

Would you rather live in a house where the furniture moves on its own or where doors and windows open and close by themselves?

Would you rather be able to talk to animals but they all tell you spooky things or be able to talk to the dead but they all want something from you?

Would you rather have the power to exorcise demons but see them everywhere or be possessed by a demon for a day?

Would you rather have a crystal ball that shows your future or a mirror that shows your past mistakes?

Would you rather be cursed to always tell the truth but no one believes you or be able to lie convincingly but always feel guilty?

Would you rather spend a week in a town where everyone is a vampire or a week in a town where everyone is a witch?

Would you rather have a ghost follow you everywhere and talk to you constantly or have a poltergeist that only makes noise at night?

Would you rather be able to predict death but not prevent it or be able to prevent death but not predict it?

Would you rather encounter a friendly ghost who wants to be your best friend or a mischievous ghost who likes to prank you?

Would you rather have a haunted doll that moves on its own or a haunted painting that changes expressions?

Would you rather be able to cast spells but have them backfire sometimes or have no magical abilities at all?

Would you rather have to perform a séance every Halloween or spend Halloween night in a cemetery alone?

Would you rather have a dream every night that predicts the next day or have a dream once a month that predicts a major event?

Would you rather have the ability to see people's auras and know their true intentions or see the spirits that haunt them?

Would you rather wake up in a haunted forest every night or a spooky, abandoned mansion every morning?

Would you rather be followed by a phantom whispering eerie secrets or a shadow that mimics your every move?

Would you rather receive cryptic messages from the afterlife or be able to send messages to the other side but never receive replies?

Would you rather have to solve a murder mystery involving a ghost or a disappearance linked to a witch's curse

Would you rather spend an hour in a room filled with possessed dolls or an hour in a room with a constantly shifting poltergeist?

Would you rather have the ability to summon spirits at will or banish them forever from your presence?

Would you rather attend a school for witches and wizards or a school for ghost hunters?

Would you rather discover your house was built on an ancient burial ground or that it was once a site for dark rituals?

Would you rather receive a visit from a ghost every Halloween or be haunted by a different supernatural creature each month?

Would you rather have your dreams controlled by an evil spirit or your waking life influenced by a mischievous ghost?

Would you rather have the power to read minds but only hear disturbing thoughts or see the future but only witness ominous events?

Would you rather be a ghost who can only haunt people you know or a ghost who can only haunt strangers?

Would you rather have the ability to time travel but be haunted by spirits from the past or have the power to foresee the future but be followed by ghosts?

Would you rather have a guardian angel who is visible to everyone or a demonic protector who only you can see?

Domestic Dillemas

Would you rather have a house that's always a little too hot or a little too cold

Would you rather have a neighbor who's constantly spying on you or one who's always throwing loud parties?

Would you rather have to clean your entire house with a toothbrush or not clean it at all?

Would you rather have a beautiful home in a terrible location or a rundown home in the perfect location?

Would you rather have to share your home with a messy roommate who never cleans or with a neat freak who's always complaining about your cleaning?

Would you rather have a luxurious bathroom with no privacy or a very basic bathroom with total privacy?

Would you rather have an amazing home gym but no living room or a fantastic living room but no bedroom?

Would you rather have to live without a refrigerator or without a stove?

Would you rather have a house that's always cluttered but smells amazing or one that's always spotless but smells bad?

Would you rather have a garden that's full of weeds but produces amazing vegetables or a perfectly manicured garden that produces nothing?

Would you rather have your dream kitchen but be unable to cook or a tiny kitchen where you're an amazing chef

Would you rather have a pool that's always too cold or a hot tub that's always too hot?

Would you rather have a home theater with no streaming services or the latest streaming services with only a small TV

Would you rather have to host a dinner party every single weekend or never be able to have guests over again?

Would you rather live in a home with no internet access or in a home where you can only watch one TV channel?

Would you rather live next to a noisy construction site for a year or beside an active train track for a year?

Would you rather have to do all your laundry by hand or never be able to use a dishwasher again?

Would you rather have a neighbor who always borrows things and never returns them or one who complains about everything you do?

Would you rather live in a house where you can hear everything your neighbors do or where they can hear everything you do?

Would you rather have a home with no electricity or one with no running water?

Would you rather have to move to a new house every year or stay in one house for the rest of your life?

Would you rather have to paint every room in your house a different neon color or have every room be pitch black?

Would you rather have a leaky roof that you can't fix or a constantly dripping faucet you can't stop?

Would you rather live in a house where the floors are always sticky or one where they're always slippery?

Hobby Hijinks

Would you rather be an amazing painter but never be able to share your work or be a terrible painter but have your work displayed everywhere?

Would you rather have to read only the same book for the rest of your life or watch only the same movie?

Would you rather have to write a novel but only using words from a children's dictionary or make a movie with a cast of only animals?

Would you rather be an amazing chef but have no sense of taste or be a terrible chef with a highly developed palate

Would you rather have to play an instrument naked at a concert or sing off-key in front of your favorite artist?

Would you rather have to create a viral dance video every week or post a highly personal blog every day?

Would you rather have to do extreme sports without any safety gear or have to participate in a beauty pageant every month?

Would you rather be the best player on a terrible team or the worst player on a championship team?

Would you rather be a famous artist who only produces one piece of work a year or a prolific artist whose work is always overshadowed by others?

Would you rather have to complete a puzzle with 1,000 pieces but no picture or build a model airplane with instructions in a foreign language?

Would you rather be known for a viral fail video or have a cringe-worthy meme about you circulate online?

Would you rather join a nudist art class as the model or as a participant?

Would you rather bake a cake shaped like an intimate body part for a family gathering or prepare an intimate dinner for your parents with an aphrodisiac menu?

Would you rather write an erotic novel published under your real name that makes thousands or a highly acclaimed poetry anthology that makes no money at all.

Would you rather have to photograph a boudoir shoot for a friend or pose in one yourself for a stranger?

Would you rather paint a nude portrait of someone you know or have someone you know paint a nude portrait of you?

Would you rather be caught reading a steamy romance novel in public or have your internet search history projected for everyone to see?

Historical Hilarity

Would you rather travel back in time and meet your ancestors or travel to the future and meet your descendants?

Would you rather have to fight in a medieval battle or navigate the political intrigue of an ancient royal court?

Would you rather have to explain modern technology to a famous historical figure or learn to live without any technology in a past era?

Would you rather attend a gladiator match in ancient Rome or a jousting tournament in medieval Europe?

Would you rather be a pirate in the Golden Age of Piracy or a cowboy in the Wild West?

Would you rather dine with Henry VIII and risk being beheaded or with Cleopatra and risk being poisoned?

Would you rather be a servant in a Victorian mansion or a soldier in the trenches of World War I?

Would you rather have to wear the fashions of the 18th century every day or the fashions of the 1960s?

Would you rather be accused of witchcraft during the Salem Witch Trials or be a heretic during the Spanish Inquisition?

Would you rather have to build a pyramid in ancient Egypt or construct the Great Wall of China?

Would you rather experience the Black Plague firsthand or live through the Great Depression?

Would you rather be a spy during World War II or a revolutionary during the American Revolution?

Would you rather live as a famous artist in the Renaissance but be poor or as a wealthy merchant in the Middle Ages but unknown?

Would you rather have to survive a Viking raid or a Mongol invasion?

Would you rather be a knight in medieval Europe or a samurai in feudal Japan

Would you rather travel on the Titanic and survive or witness the moon landing in person?

Would you rather have to entertain at the court of Louis XIV or perform in Shakespeare's Globe Theatre?

Would you rather experience the French Revolution or the Russian Revolution

Would you rather be a scientist during the Age of Enlightenment or an explorer during the Age of Discovery?

Would you rather live in a utopian society that eventually fails or a dystopian society that you help rebuild?

Would you rather attend a wild Roman orgy or a lavish Victorian ball where you're underdressed?

Would you rather be caught in a love triangle with Cleopatra and Julius Caesar or with Henry VIII and Anne Boleyn?

Would you rather be forced to live as a concubine in a sultan's harem or as a courtesan in 18th-century France?

Would you rather live through the hedonism of the Roaring Twenties or the paranoia of the McCarthy era?

Would you rather have to navigate a scandalous affair with Marie Antoinette or get involved in political intrigue with Catherine the Great?

Reality TV Ridiculousness

Would you rather compete on a dating show where all your exes are contestants or on a talent show where you have no talent?

Would you rather be the first to get eliminated on a reality competition or make it to the finals but lose in a humiliating way?

Would you rather live in a house with strangers for a month with cameras everywhere or be followed by a reality TV crew for a year?

Would you rather win a survival challenge by eating something disgusting or by completing a physically grueling task

Would you rather have a public meltdown on a reality TV show or get caught on camera doing something illegal?

Would you rather be the villain everyone loves to hate on a reality show or the forgettable nice person who gets no screen time?

Would you rather have to fake a relationship on a dating show or have a real relationship implode on TV?

Would you rather be stuck in a reality show with your least favorite family member or with your most annoying coworker?

Would you rather win a cash prize on a game show but everyone thinks you cheated or lose but everyone thinks you played honorably?

Would you rather participate in a makeover show where you have to wear ridiculous outfits or a cooking show where you have no idea how to cook?

Would you rather be forced to reveal a deep personal secret on live TV or have an embarrassing video of you go viral?

Would you rather be part of a reality show where you're always scared (haunted house, paranormal activities) or one where you're always grossed out (eating bugs, messy challenges)?

Would you rather have to perform a ridiculous task in front of a live audience or sing karaoke badly on national TV?

Would you rather be on a reality show where you have to lie to win or one where you have to tell the truth no matter what?

Would you rather be on a dating show where you have to date someone your parents chose or date someone chosen by your ex?

Would you rather be on a reality show where you compete in embarrassing challenges for money or one where you compete in dangerous stunts for fame?

Would you rather have a reality show filmed in your messy home or at your embarrassing workplace?

Would you rather win a reality TV show but become infamous or lose but become beloved by the audience?

Would you rather have to live in a remote location with no amenities for a reality survival show or in a luxury mansion with the most annoying people for a reality drama show?

Would you rather be on a reality show where you have to eat bizarre foods or one where you have to live with bizarre people?

Parental Perplexities

Would you rather have your toddler throw a tantrum in the middle of a quiet library or during a packed movie theater?

Would you rather have to explain where babies come from to a group of kids or discuss the birds and the bees with your teenager?

Would you rather deal with a toddler who refuses to potty train or a teenager who refuses to clean their room?

Would you rather have your child repeat your most embarrassing moment in front of your in-laws or in front of your boss

Would you rather find out your child has been bullying someone or that they are being bullied?

Would you rather have to attend every parents' meeting in a clown costume or have to volunteer to be part of the PTA?

Would you rather your teenager walk in on you having sex or walk in on them?

Would you rather have to eat only your child's favorite foods for a month or have them eat only your least favorite foods for a month?

Would you rather deal with a baby who never stops crying or a teenager who never stops talking back?

Would you rather have to homeschool your child for a year or work as a janitor at their school for a year?

Would you rather have your child throw up in your new car or on your brand-new couch?

Would you rather have to listen to your child's favorite song on repeat for a week or watch their favorite TV show non-stop for a week?

Would you rather have your child bring home lice or a contagious stomach bug?

Would you rather have to sit through your child's four-hour school play or a two-hour recital of their least favorite instrument?

Would you rather have your child ask you an awkward question in public or have them embarrass you with a loud comment about someone else?

Would you rather deal with a toddler who throws food at every meal or a teenager who refuses to eat anything but junk food?

Would you rather have to read the same bedtime story every night for a year or listen to your child's favorite bedtime song on repeat every night for a year?

Crossing the Line
(Yah.. we're going there)

Would you rather confess to your partner about a one-time infidelity or find out they've been cheating on you for years

Would you rather have to tell your parents about your kinkiest sexual fantasy or listen to theirs?

Would you rather have a video of you getting blackout drunk go viral or have a video of you in a compromising sexual position shared between your close friends?

Would you rather be caught by your in-laws while having sex or catch your in-laws having sex?

Would you rather have a coworker find your secret stash of sex toys or accidentally email a sexy photo to your entire office?

Would you rather walk in on your best friend cheating on their partner or have them walk in on you cheating on yours?

Would you rather tell your partner you're not sexually satisfied or hear them tell you the same?

Would you rather participate in a public orgy or have your sexual history published in a popular magazine?

Would you rather find out your partner is a sex worker or find out your parent is?

Would you rather have a threesome with two people you work with and will see every day or two people you find unattractive?

Would you rather accidentally send a dirty text to a family member or receive a dirty text from a family member?

Would you rather walk in on your best friend cheating on their partner or have them walk in on you cheating on yours?

Would you rather tell your partner you're not sexually satisfied or hear them tell you the same?

Would you rather participate in a public orgy or have your sexual history published in a popular magazine?

Would you rather find out your partner is a sex worker or find out your parent is?

Would you rather have a threesome with two people you work with and will see every day or two people you find unattractive?

Would you rather accidentally send a dirty text to a family member or receive a dirty text from a family member?

Would you rather find out your partner had a one-night stand or that they've been having an emotional affair for months?

Would you rather have a sex tape leak during a family gathering or during a work meeting?

Would you rather swap sexual fantasies with your best friend or your sibling?

Would you rather participate in a reality show about your sex life or have to perform a sex act in front of a live audience?

Would you rather find out your parents are swingers or that they have a secret porn collection featuring themselves?

Would you rather have your nudes leaked by a hacker or by an ex with a grudge?

The end... or just the beginning?

You've navigated through the hilarious, awkward, and absurd world of "Would You Rather?" We hope you had as much fun playing as we had creating these scenarios.

Whether you have laughed in mortification, discovered something new about your friends, or simply enjoyed the absurdity of it all, thank you for being a part of this wild ride.

Remember, life is full of choices – some are easy, some are tough, and some are downright ridiculous. Embrace the laughter, cherish the moments of honesty, and never shy away from a little bit of outrageous fun.

Until Next Time...

Made in the USA
Monee, IL
22 December 2024

75224052R00057